Words From The Shadows

Selection of works by Robert Young

Gratitude and Dedication

Grace, Tanya. M,
Andrew, Dave, and Guin

ISBN:9798338828007

Copyright © 2024 Robert Young.
All Rights Reserved.

No part of this publication may be reproduced, distributed, or transmitted in any form or by any means, including photocopying, recording, or other electronic or mechanical methods, or by any information storage and retrieval system without the prior written permission of the publisher, except in the case of very brief quotations embodied in critical reviews and certain other non-commercial uses permitted by copyright law.

At the age of 9 or 10 I had a head injury. On a fast and steep hill, went over the top of the handlebars of a borrowed pushbike, and landed on my head. Rushed to hospital, I was unconscious for days. I'm not sure how long, it could have been a week but was probably 3 or 4 days. The reflexes in my legs were messed up and I spend a long time in recovery both in and out of hospital. During this recovery time I forgot how to read. My Mum tried to encourage me to read whilst convalescing in bed, but the strain on my eyes hurt and with a constant throbbing headache.

When I eventually went back to school, I had to do lots of extra out of school classes. Meg Southwell taught me for years to get better at reading writing and spelling. After 3 years of 2 sessions a week she tested me and announced with much disappointment that I was still 2 years behind where I should be.
I was devastated and despondent.
When I was about 13, I overheard Meg saying that she would always mark people down so they would be motivated to students try harder. It had the opposite effect on me. Profound it was.

Sometime in my early teens I was also diagnosed with dyslexia.
I cared not for any kind of schoolwork. My friends took the piss out of me at school, I wrote 'mental' as opposed to 'metal'. They had much delight, and rightfully so. Years later in my mid-thirties I realised that I don't read words

phonetically,

I look at the shape of the word and see if it fits. The words were filed in my brain in shapes not alphabetically. It was a bit tricky. I'm told this is not uncommon. A revelation, a filing cabinet full of shaped words.

I worked as a photographer and had a lovely client called Virginia. I was diligent with all my correspondence and avid religious spell checker.
Which I did.
      Dear Vagina

www.RobertYoung.com.au

Warning and suggestion.
Some topics expressed in these works are dark and heavy.

If you're feeling like you may become overwhelmed with dark subjects. Please put the to one side until you are able.

General suggestion; Read one or 2 works per day.

Contents

Will It Offend	11
My Mind	13
Colour Be Gone	14
Close Of Play	15
Roberts Love	17
Cigarette	19
Gaunt	20
Beaches	21
Burnt	22
Do you?	23
Modern God	27
Its ridiculous	29
The illness of being	32
Life on any other day	34
Today's not the day	36
and I still haven't found you	39
The Threat	42
Who Knew	43
The Quite Embrace	45
ageing	46
Homophobic houses	47
can I	50
ejb	52
synonym	53
Acid.doc	54
This Time With More Feeling	57
Hold Deep	58
NIPPLE	60
Sorry's	61
Two Goes	62
Puce Face	64

you speak not	65
It's Just a Lie	66
Everyday	68
The Waitress	71
Meek	72
…..as in penguin	73
Trust	74
Trust – Bar – Three	75
Better Door	76
Where are you	78
Best I ever had, But I could do better	82
EveryThing	84
A two wank night	85
She is dead, long live She	87
New towns edgy wash	90
Not Too Bad	93

Will It Offend

Will it offend
if I have sex
with my best friend?

Is it wrong
to sleep with my
guardian of spirit?

Is it
an error
to make love
with my heroine?

Is it just not done
coitus ET all
with my saviour ?

am I a fool
to fall in love
with this pedestal ?

is it
contrite
to fuck
my shining light ?

Is it
obtuse of course
to enjoy intercourse
with this Priestess ?

is it wrong to inscribe
my inflamed arousal
on my intimate counsel ?

is it contrary
to sly a leer at
the curve
of my divinity ?

cos I do

My Mind

My mind
        has a mind of its own

Colour Be Gone

And colour be gone
I coloured in
      the indifference
I coloured in
      the flaws, the frailty and the fantastical
I coloured in
      the feeling, the meaning and the sincerity
I coloured in
      my place in your world
and colour be gone

I coloured in
      the future with child like gusto
I coloured in
      the feelings that didn't fit
I coloured in
      the love you offered
I coloured in
      you
colour be gone

your madness
      my attraction
your dysfunction
      so insatiable
your honesty
      my novelty
            hidden in your arm
                  and colour be gone

Close Of Play

No let's wrap this up
and unpack it
can you speak to it
and put lipstick on the pig

The take away is
it is what it is
and, moving forward
this I promise you, it really has legs

The fact if the matter is
we'll touch base
To connect the dots
and we'll need to pull the pin to push the envelope

Let's see if we have bandwidth
and line all our ducks in a row
we'll get the low hanging fruit
that thinks outside the box

If we run it up the flag pole
we can raise the bar
and stay in the loop
in any way, shape, or form

It really gets me triggered.
comparing apples to apples
we're getting some push back,
from the elephant in the room

Start with a clean slate
to polish this turd
but its good to put a face to the name
just read my lips, who moved my cheese?

The light at the end of the tunnel
was thrown under the bus
let's park that for while
and colour inside the lines to reinvent the wheel

Will you drill down
to the helicopter view
and parachute it in
to a perfect storm, cos we're facing significant headwinds

Its a real game changer
to drop the ball
I'm a team player
and I'm not sure we have enough boots on the ground

We need to wrap our heads around this
long story short
people upstairs like it
and boys will be boys at the big end of town

At the end of the day
when all's said and done.
You can't have your cake and eat it,
you'll need to step up to the plate and face the music

Roberts Love

can I hang my art on your walls
and waft with some virtue
do you want some water for bed
and can I have your Wi-Fi password
can I ?

can I dis-guard my socks on your floor
and hang my art on your walls
can I wash my hands in your sink
and riffle intently for a glass
can I mix my underwear in your washing
and abandon spent plates on the side
can I ?

can I thumb through and expose your fridge
and yet park in your garage
can I park in your garage
and smile at your neighbours
can I test out your best seat
and sense your underwear draw
can I ?

can I wee in your shower
and hang my art on your walls
Can I smell your sheet
and fluff your pillow
can I set the mood
and choose the next tune
can I?

can I show you something new
a show off trick to entice you
can I park in your garage
and put my toothbrush next to yours
can I sink and mellow into your sofa
and put my art in your walls
can I?

Cigarette

you wear Robert Smith's cigarette burn
        with pride but
                not me

you say you're falling in love
        but not
                with me

you offer sorry
        but its just words
                for me

you text the apology
        that speaks so little
                to me
and that feels more
        like a typo
                to me

you're shine
        has no light
                for me

your kind
        is not kind
                to me

Gaunt

Gaunt with loss and void
The bland and mass franchised
all-most alive
sway to the next outlet trough.
Faux vinyl, imitation food and
screaming discounts,
lecture us on culture.
The all-dead come here.
The weekly dose of avoidance
Rejoicing in skin deep shallowness of 1/2 price and get a second pair free
Gaunt with void and loss
The franchisable trudge aimlessly
and amass at the next trough
Satisfied with the empty smile
of capitalism
just doing it's thing

Beaches

she shall doggedly go on to the end
she shall fight in the courts
she shall fight with the underhanded and trickery
she shall fight with growling bitterness
and growling strength in the her ways
she shall lack the truth, whatever the cost

she shall fight me on the beaches
she shall fight me on the school grounds
she shall fight me in the messages, and in the streets
she shall fight me in the hills
she shall never surrender

she shall sacrifice the offspring
and throw it under the tram
she shall discredit
with lies and warm wet harm
she shall fight me in the offspring and of their friends
she shall fight on door steps
she shall fight me on the beaches
for she can never surrender

Burnt

fingers been burnt
got too close
money's sexy smile
········lured me into compromise

Do you?

Do you get a tingle
with the vulnerable?
Do you find tears
arousing?
Do you bide your time
to linger a feel?
      Is there room
        to groom?

Do you get overrun
when they are overcome?
Do you force
well past awkward?
Do you dream
of when they scream?
Or do you like them paralysed
white with fear?

      Do you?

Do you angle your position
so you can better your glimpse?
Do you like to wrestle
and mask your thrust?
Do you offer kind words
with expensive connotations?
Do you like to intoxicate
disarm, disable and placate

      Do you ?

Do you thrive with the possibilities
of the changing rooms?
Do you get ruttish
when in their bedroom?
Do you accidentally rest your hand
or go straight and cop a feel?
Do you try and kiss
or ignore the face?

      Do you?

Do you get righteous
when you overpower?
Do you get all flush
when you restrain?
Do you get a rush
with the gaze of terror?

      Do you?

Do you smile at your victim?
In that knowing way
do you give a pat on the back?
to keep it all updated
do you wink at your victim?
its our little big secret

      Is there room
      to groom?

Do you justify your actions
with they asked for it?

Do you justify your actions
with it never happened?

do you hide behind your religion,
your stature,
and your job
do you hide behind
it happened to me
do you hide behind
I was drunk

>	Is there room
>	to groom?
>
>	Is there room
>	to groom?
>
>	Is there room
>	to groom?

Pause Page

Modern God

The Beatles are more popular that God.
Social media is more popular than God.
Cocaine is more popular than God.

The lord is my god
and my god is speaking
PLEASE be quite
please be quite in this place of worship

I love you my god
my morning vice
your rich smell
your warm touch and glowing on a cold day

disciples come from far and wide
to devote and be with you
to enjoy your peace and contemplation
to furnish the little addiction-tradition

the congregation drink
the blood of christ
some pray at hand held screens and some eat
the body of christ

pilgrimage in one's, two's and three's
to be by your side at mass
and discuss the incidentals or repent sins
and seek comfort with you on their lips

the lord is god
with you in my veins
I clasp my hands and together we pray
the lord is my god
I shall not want

Its ridiculous

Its ridiculous she said.
I wasn't so sure.
Smile. I did.

Don't you worry about that
she said.
but I did
I said.

Its our anniversary
she said.
but it wasn't.
I knew.

it would be an honour she said.
made me all king like.
Inside. I was.

Give me your cum she said
and I spat in her eye.
I did.

Its our song she said.
but I don't do our song
I said.

She was honest
she said.
I wasn't sure.
And, didn't say.

I just had to have you
she said.
Oh, I said.

Lets mooch I said.
I love mooching she said.
So we did.

She met my gaze she did.
I read her well.
I did.

She hated my friends
she did.
All jealous.
All knotted she did

We, we got this she said.
My heart sang.
It did

She drank she did
she lost the plot.
She did

I gave her my script I did.
Help her see me,
but didn't.

The sun shone from her
it did,
bit cracked it was.

Cooked me breakfast, she did.
Healthy and loved,
it was.

She tied my shoes she did
but sometimes knots,
it was.

Lavish she was.
I needed real,
I did

Broken hearted, I am,
months past
that is.

Cant pick the phone. I cant.
Scared of repeats
I am.

Scared of repeats
I am.

Scared of repeats
I am.

Scared of repeats
I am.

The illness of being

my heart thumping
rushing air collects my face
calming to an 80 motorcycles
per hour

beside me a big over-necessary-four-wheeled-drive
hogging too much tired black tarmac
having just pushed me from my lane
emergency fashion
to the next

along side
my disdain frothing at my mouth
all taught in my lips
I stare and stare
the driver oblivious
the driver content with freedom and dominance

in the back seat glancing at me
a girl sits, also oblivious
in my eyes.
This is the daughter of the devil
the offending is genetic

Our eyes meet.
Without hesitation
I violate the wind with a gesture
I stick my prize finger to meet her

she gasps in shock
and slaps her hand to her mouth
eyes wide
and I too
gasp in disbelief at my actions

I seek to repent my sins
I seek to make amends
I seek to offer my sadness to
the 10 year old back-seat-girl

back-seat-girl will never know
back-seat-girl never knew her mother is a potential killer
back-seat-girl now believes motorcyclists are violent
back-seat-girl now knows the world is scary

the inability to exist without damage
my killing of an ant with a hammer
the tar brush that splatters all
the brutality of being

Life on any other day

tight clothes walks
past
flickering eyes toward me
demanding some notice, feeding some void
or just because

hunched and gaunt set of bones
searches for a juicy butt
to savour later
in a quite needed moment

mother doing her best
pushing the pram that feeds it
admiral in her persistence
testing the very nature of persistence like never she knew

the old swagger of a set of loafers
pass by, boat like with me in its wash
these long shorts meet high socks
that's paced so far in this life

child haunts a pigeon, all smiles
around the steps and over the path.
again admiral mother
patiently awaits to the side, sipping coffee

two wheeled whizzy
dives between coffee waiters and the pedestrians
while big carrying tradies exclaims
MIND YOUR BACKS !

the morning sets to a work stride
equalled by the passion of the work,
or the clock
mostly unconsidered blurry trudge
or the mission of a submarine

a startlingly bright council worker
happy in his world, shuts part of the path
with danger warning cones,
for cleaning is needed
complete with those coffee cups
       and juicy butts
              lost forever

Today's not the day

I haven't cleaned up
I cant leave this chaos to others
and I haven't finished my will
today's not the day
today's not the day
but this minute hurts more than most
if I can just move this minute
to another minute
replace it with a distraction
then this minute will not be here

today's not the day
and I wont talk about the future
and I wont talk about my responsibility
and I wont talk about the guilt
But its this minute you see

today's not the day
the things I can't face
I cant face tomorrow
today's a perfect day

today's not the day
but its close
its always close
even when we went our separate ways,
remember that,
you knew where I lived
you knew my mother
you knew my number

today's not the day
said with hate
with equal anger and victim resignation
and a past that can kill and elephant
today's not the fucking day

Pause Page

and I still haven't found you

yes true
underwater
over water
in a sauna
and one mile up

and I still haven't found you

in a forest
up a tree
on the beach
and
the main exhibit

but I
haven't found you

I've had intercourse before first course
obviously shagged in a shag-pile
made love on the love rug
I've got it on and had it off
I've banged
I've bonked
I've humped

but where are you ?

bragging and true
cunnilingus king
the midas man
a great cock
its a stonker
and gold fingers
but how did you do that ?
are my private mantle piece trophies

but I still haven't found you

and
only oral
please, anal
me on top !
HARDER-FASTER-MORE
can I piss on you ?
(hummm, a new boundary)

and yet
I still haven't found you

hit me
slap me
call me slut
pull my hair
tie me up and tie me down

is this the way to find you ?

copulate
conjugate
penetrate
ejaculate
and over rate

but where are you?

The Threat

just fuck off
or
I'll turn you
into a poem

Who Knew

shalamit
shalamit
shall we do the fan-dan-go?

Who knew
the thrift in your kiss
who knew
being your new favourite human being
was not worth the air it was spoken on

who knew
you cant love

who knew
my pillow talk was your latest currency for latte
conversations
who knew
my dark and private
was a gallery collection for your use

who knew
you cant love

who knew
my new best friend was so fleeting
who knew
I'm in love, is as empty as a poor mans wallet

who knew
you broken love

who knew
you'd return my love gifts
second hand, used and unwanted
who knew
these words would be for you

who knew?

The Quite Embrace

We learned a new language
naturally and effortlessly
and spoke in nods gleams and cues
understandably and silently
words used for the pure enjoyment and delight
with pure delight in the words and in the sights

two peas in a pod
me the Mary
and you the bloody

me the you
bloody the Mary

you offered me home
I offered you loyalty

the quiet embrace of no contact

ageing

as she forgets
I
remember

Homophobic houses

Oversized and self-righteous
glossy cock-swinging brand-new four-wheel drives
litter this no man's land.
With its undercurrent,
mine is bigger than yours.

Crass mass soulless products
franchised laden outlets compound this postcode
where style is a purchase
of cheap or ostentatious, and better still, both.
My ignorance is bigger than yours.

The over whelming tyrant's expression of thuggery
honed over red meat, car loans, over extended mortgages
unhappy marriages and dysfunctional communication
ingrain the face.
My shit life is bigger than yours.

Sudden yet unsurprising vicious playground street brawls
blood drawn
expose the brittle self-importance.
Self-importance bonded to the self-entitlement.
And my self-entitlement is bigger than yours

Modern glass and steel palaces
sit acute, showy, expensive and unnecessary
devised to hide the hollow within.
For my shallowness is hollower than yours.

Burning desires of nightly hangings from street lamps
dangle Abbos, Muslims, or Greenies.
Social cleansing is as good as it gets
and mask the insecurity that is
mine, just has to be bigger than yours.

Years by, the vague intelligent school's bully
that contribute their threat, 'you know I'm a solicitor'
and the less intelligent
enters the world of building thug and menace.
My oblivious distress is bigger than yours.

Vulgar Homophobic houses, built
from pictures on disposable social media
where sexual coerce is disguised by drunkenness
scream cock is king
and hide the secret longing for anal sex
For my intolerance is bigger than yours.

Tuesday night's the boss has asked me to work back late night
lie the secret hand-job, blow-job or fuck-a-slut.
While wives hold sex as their weapon of choice.
For my sex play is more one sided.

'Your not respecting my property'
barks with bile, the neighbour,
'you parked in-front of my house'
the blood socked words fume of anger
meet the guise.
My cocks not hard anymore.

With keep em out, lock em up
embed the rich right wing pungent views
wafts through the air like the smell of a
down trodden corner pub at opening time.
And my self medication is more needed than yours

Women are possessions
kids are accessories
lesbians are for wanking over
and religion is for keeping it all strapped together.
For my sanctuary is nowhere and here.

Anger splashed out all
over the car-park
'she's parked like a cunt'
and the twinge of an erection over the
sprue of bile just released.
For my delusion is bigger than yours.

Only 8 siren miles from the city,
compete on its face of neat trimmed grass
regimented scented trees and gardens
hiding the scathing pit of the stomach.
For my god awful life is more awful than yours.

can I

can I sit next to you?
just to be here
can I stand here?
to be your counted
can we count together?
and face it
can you stand next to me?
sometimes I'm scared
can you tell me your stories?
because yours seems so important
can I walk with you?
and amble along this path
can I tell you my story?
my dark, my shame and glory
can I listen to your heart
and what it says?
can I capture those butterflies
and mount them for the wall?
can I take your breath away
and treasure the memento?
can I smell your scent?
so it all makes sense
can I show you my fear
and the map out of here?

can you hold my hopes
and open them when I need?
can I have your back?

and can I sit next to you?

20th Sept 2019
Sharon RIP

ejb

you never swayed
you always endured
        what she gave
        what she dealt out

you never swayed
you never used force.
        for what she did
        for what she said

you never swayed
just capitulate
emasculate
against this heavyweight
        in her fail
        and her betrayal

synonym

≥ synonym
\> no meaning found

Acid.doc

you are the
Mexican wave ME TOO shouts
an early age Harvey
a practising Crosby

for you are the drug-er
you are the saddest sadist.
what fun, as I lose my mind
and what fun for you, I lose my name

I saw you
You know, I know
I hold my tongue
until this ME TOO finds its way

For you roll with role models
not for sex and rape
more disturbed, more sadistic
just to humiliate, head fuck

your distant skyward dismissing rye grin
and your facade of everyone is my friend
'no you finish the joint',
from that other sly acid jacket pocket
that Michael Jackson big shoulder padded imitation

I saw blind, as I do
my vile bad choice friend
I over looked,
your insecurity, your nervous twitch and that prized silly accent

You sit head of the small cock table
and command service from your dutiful wife object
and play your small cock games
with glints your ego flashing

and who are you anyway ? You ask
I'm the one to haunt you
the one to linger in your mind
You are the one that no words can repay

I just didn't give it the consideration I should have
spoken in perfect upper class plumb English
words full of potential, and devoid of meaning
the story of your life

and the ME TOO shouts
you store friends addictions escapades and tales
and use them as currency.
yes please take down that karma in the mirror

Betrayal everywhere
every lasting relationship betrayed for cheep currency.
you are a spy from the enemy of friend-ship
I'll never hold your currency
but id trade you for a simple smile off a destitute any-day.

I takes 40 years to write this
and sort this
but this it is
this is you
this is your legacy

are you as bad as a Harvey?
Are you like a Cosby, a Jimmy, David?
just the non sexual perversion version?

I curse you to the end of time
may lonely walk through your veins
may heart ache rest in your soul

This Time With More Feeling

This time with more feeling
see all that water under the bridge ?
I notice your seven and eights
reminds me of times past

have you ever had rain on your face and sun in your eyes
this time with more feeling
So much water   so much bridge
its enough for one
            thanks!

you notice
        I, forever humbled.
and have you ever jumped without knowing?

this time
with more feeling.
are we the water ?
or are we the bridge ?

noticing the unnoticed is everything
I embrace this love
This time with more feeling

Hold Deep

And everything I hold deep
and everything I hold deeper
and every feeling I ever had
and everything I never had

you made some of the answers clearer

and again I feel you
and again I need you
and again I hide from you
and again I don't know you

you made some clear cloudy

and all the time I shone for you
and all the time I spoke for you
and all the time I held you tight
and all the time I loved you

you made some of the dead awake again

and all of the newness
and all of the brightness
and all of the thoughtlessness
and all of the hopelessness

and you made some more hope

and always stuck in my throat
and always when I tie my shoe
and always in the middle of a second
and always between a thought

you always did that

and even when
and even then
and even why
and even you

did you even do that

and more than ever
and more than now
and more than this
and more than, can I ?

you more than time

and every one
and every time
and every look
and every even

you held some of my oxygen

and always even more
and every feeling was
and every more even
and all that was

I hold deep

NIPPLE

offer me your nipple
to my sweet and innocent lips
let me give you
your motherhood
so deserved
woon me with the warmth
and regulate my heart

Sorry's

I just,
I just wonder if there are enough Sorry's?
Sorry's for you.
Sorry's for me.
Stored in the prestigious Sorry places and Sorry palaces.
A royal pardon, is that the same?

I just,
I just, i have a bronze account at the Sorry palace.
First name terms with the Sorry receptionist.
It's her first job since leaving school.
Sorry state of affairs.
They come in too, trying to reconcile their affairs.
But not me, I'm here for the regular Sorry.

I just,
I just think
it's all she's known, you know.
People walking in with heads bowed low
'Can I withdraw a Sorry', they all say in low tones,
withdrawal slips in Sorry hand.
What will happen with internet Sorry withdrawals?
Just txt them ?

Two Goes

If I hold my breath will I stop ?
If I held my breath will it stop ?
If I hold this will it go ?
Will it fester?
Will it go faster,
        if I blink ?

I just
I just hide my eyes
and miss a bit
No one will notice
No notice will be penned and pinned
I just eyes my hide
For a bittle lit
        (dyslexia intended)

I just
I just want two goes
One for
my
emotions to do their run
and
the second to react how I would,
like.
I just
I just want two lives
A dry run,
And
a wet one
but, should the wet one should go first ?

I just
I just want two attempts
I'm sure I can get it,
right?
Right-wrong-right-left
left-wrong-left-up-down-left-downside-up-left,
right?

Puce Face

Puce pus ooze face
flannel tage mit-tism
pain-stained cloth killed mace
define all things nice

muck smear gutter waste
putrid mirror reflections
disposable provocative adverbs
moist of all colour

phlegm and air part lips
flaps mucus and dribble in texts
bap slurp scrape slope
dysfunction renal squat you say

flaccid curd and pantie cysts
gusset retarded pustules
galloping so proud
yet gushing secretion so loud

vomit squaller you preach
pulpit discharge like green snot
barren to the soul
barren and toxic

you speak not

I speak not
you speak not
I hide with speak not
and act out intuition
act out superstition
you speak not

you hide out in speak not
offer deception deflection or embarrassment
indifference or lone
I hide in speak not

clearly I'm not
clearly you're not

speak not

It's Just a Lie

Dear Mr TimeWillTell
firstly thank you
for meeting with me,
all those months
ago.

I must however
and
regrettably inform
you that my heart,
the one that
was
extended to you has
been returned
with some
damage attached.

The meeting,
our meeting
seemed to go well,
well, as well as expected,
until the end.

You see
Mr TimeWillTell
I didn't
say you're an unkind person
I didn't
say that I wanted you out of my life
I said you never
praise or encourage
but sneak the snide critique.

And time told me
Mr TimeWillTell,
ungraciously.

I'm sorry I hurt you
enough for you
to build a space
big enough
for me to view
the gulf
with binoculars
and wander across this space
with emptiness.
Take care.
Point taken.
It seems you won't be.
sorry and good-bye.

Everyday

Everyday
you walk with me
and every day
you shadow me

the dark and days end
and i please your flay

Everyday
you tint my dream
and every day
i glow in your verve

the rich stained peace
and i bask in your solace

Everyday
you watch me, and wait
and every day
I hold your hand

you, the thief borrow my make
and I let you

Everyday
you ex-girlfriend me
and every day
I pay

you smell familiar
and unfair
with you on my back

Everyday
you invite yourself in
and every day
we play cards

you enjoy the shine of light
and you enjoy the shine of light
that's all you have
and that's all you'll have

for M

Pause Page

The Waitress

No don't smile
don't look that way at me
for I
am, too easily confused
I like you
your smile
your hair
and
well
if you
smile
I'm confused, between
the gift of a tip
and my narcissism

Meek

The meek shall inherit the world
                    still fucking waiting!

                        Clearly not meek

…..as in penguin

guin, you said

as in pen-guin
not like
ruin
ru-in
as in
ru-ined
Eternal and Unfathomable

Trust

I trust you with a million dollars
I trust you with my naked daughter……

I wrote the start of this poem about David Kelso. I became stumped by the fact that I only could count one other male, my cousin, Andrew Bilsdon that I could attribute these qualities. (I have, since thought of another, my ex father in law, Colin Scope another good man).

I'm disturbed with the fact that I can only think of 2 (now 3) males that I would trust at this level, in the world.
Is it the quality of people I know ?
Is this just a too big an ask ?
Or is it that we just don't furnish a society where trust is a basic principle of life?

I also, contemplate if someone could attribute the same trust to me ?

Young men are often left without great guidance to either being trustworthy person or how to treat women, I look back on my late teen years and early twenties and am guilty of not being that honourable, often exercising my desire or feelings over being completely honourable. I filled in lots of the gaps with B-Grade titillating American collage films where the sub plot is all about the male getting sex. And seen as acceptably so.

The accessibility to porn and how that must be infusing young minds is a important reflection on what we allow to be acceptable.
Porn is not love, and love is not in porn.
We rarely trust the Media, Politicians and leaders of industry. Politicians don't practice what they preach and are seldom true leaders.
Environmentally we've not respected our earth. Bit like cancer. If we furnish the world with platforms that enable misinformation surely this is a cancer on our civilisation.

Trust – Bar – Three

I don't trust 4,148,389,727 males with a million dollars
and,
I don't trust them with my naked daughter
Bar – Three.

Better Door

Where mattresses take pride of place
on grass verges
Where once gleaming furniture
was never meant to grow past puberty

Where car tyres seek permanent
old timer spots beside some lamppost
Where gnarly dogs bark someplace in the background
for no reason

A push bike, once full of smiles
sits buckle-wheeled, seat missing, gently returns to rust
Where an ill sense of peace
gets regularly shattered by screams coming from them,
again

Where employment is hard to find
and commitment harder
Whilst force-ably exposed to the glossy glory of life
never to be realised

Where relationships are brimming with expectation
and understood emotion are foggy at best
Where moral corruption
is as destitute as the cu-de-sac

Where the heart strings are tugged
and the have-nots give more
They know the price to pay
the price of pain and the price of shame

Where the frequently damaged come to rest their head
or hide behind the crack or the smack
or wine by the bottle one or two
do the washing tomorrow

Where behind the fence becomes the breading ground
unwanted underage babies
looked after by unwanted underage babies
Life imitating life

Skyla get inside
echoes off concrete
and more money is spent on the sleeve
than the education

Where cars propped up by bricks
a modern day still life, in the front yard
Keen and eager for a new go
quietly screams out of hope lost

and is this the best we can do
is the grand sum of the human pace
and is the best we can do
to help the slow runners

Can we not point the pointy end
to flourish the bandaged
can we not divert the race for greed
and provide keys for a better door

Where are you

Robert Endersby
last seen making jewellery for the Eurythmics
all moley, blubber rubber lipped and a deep wicked laugh.
burning a hole in my vinyl record, from all accounts

Where are you ?

And where are you
Freddy Laver
last seen drumming for Ten Pole Tuder
small and sub-adult but wanted to grow fast.
And did
Lived life with a user stance.
Where are you ?

And where are you
Steve Gooding
lost to time, haunting dad's death
a river of rebellion, with nameless infanticide
last heard pimping out girls, but I don't believe that
Where are you Steve ?

Did you have a happy life ?
Success brio bro
And love, is it a good story?

And where are you
Paul Hocking
the coolest punk, with a smile that could bed anyone
Synex member, last seen heading to smack and Brighton
Where are you ?

Terry Johns where are you
you taught me all about anarchy in the Hope & Anchor
and your brother Shawn
that thundered CUNT to me and my mother that day
punks v teddy boys, honest tribal small mindedness

Dave Gorum
I hope you dead dead dead man.
Never met evil, but I think you may be it
I SAW you follow that girl into the park.
I hope you're dead dead dead.

And where are you
Ralph Levet
with a hard start to life
and such a defiant stance, you made me smile
castrating Stumpy Styles and my god your golfing handy cap.
Where are you ?

And you big Bumble Seal
butcher by trade, musician by love
cornered me, no place to hide and too scared to sing
am I here and you there
are you still alive ?

Paul Nutt, where are you
funny smiley guy, full of chronic disobedience
Saw inside of borstal with bad teeth
never safe, could change mood faster than flick a cigarette butt
Where are you ?

William Tucker, where oh where are you Tucker ?
bones held together with luck
teeth imported from an adult
bullied but happy
where are you ?

Have you a happy ?
Successes bro ?
And your love story?

Where are you Stuart Matthews
an amateur Rothmans smoker, with divorced parents
straight laced with stoned smiles and a odd gait
XTC record playing in the background whilst having nookie
What became of you ?

John Wright, I know where you are.
Just hiding round the corner and in the next room
your intrigued zest, and youthful free wheeler
and that middle parting with split lip
RIP John

Murray Keyley, I'm guessing you didn't make it much
beyond 20
the love of being smashed, alcohol, breaking into chemists
and finding park benches
brilliant mind devoted to non connection with it

Liam McGauley are you still in en-ger-land ?
proud importer of the IRA
hated deformity, hated motorcycles
crashed and you can guess the rest.
give him my best

and where are you Sam Williamson
actually your not worth words

and you cant be still alive Mr Cannon
all upright and bearded complete with corporal
punishment
taught me the world can mind blowing
where its all very possible
Thank-you Mr Cannon

was is a good life worth living ?
Were you OK with the reflection in the mirror
And love, was your heart full ?

Pierre Williams, so did you go to prison ?
last seen in The Chequers
telling me all about the guns
he had
or wanted
or used
or some such.
I used to bike ride with you
and steal away to stare at Penthouse
Are you there, somewhere ?

Martin Thorpe, what happened
you and Grant become a inseparable mixture
of the bad and the unhealthy
I imagine you being head cunt at some fucker
corporation now
Are you?

Michael Platts, Where are you ?
Honest the day is long.
Saved my life. No really.
We stole your dads blue mags, remember ?
I hope you had a great life
my friend

Best I ever had, But I could do better

every breath you take
I wont be watching you

correction, we didn't have words
you bruised bruised and abused

someday, my disdain
will be a distant stain

it will take long dry winters
too fill this bare plundered heart

too re-coat
and fill the gaps

yet overhaul
and hide the cracks

I probably think this poem as about me
don't I ?
I probably think this poem as about me
don't I ?

I refuse to write vitriol
I refuse to make what was, into anything, but was.

and every step you take
I wont be there.

everyday the truth lays
somewhere between the breaths
and saying you could do better
and every claim you stake

I won't believe you
and I don't believe in you

EveryThing

I'm everything
you ever dreamt of
but real

A two wank night

Its like, you know,
a 2 wank night
One was not enough
Its a 2 wank night last night.

I didn't have this thought to start
of a 2 wank night,
just something wasn't right
on this 2 wank night last night.

I had a nice day, nothing special
this beige 2 wank night last night.
One didn't hit the spot
and yet the second one, done in a jot.

Not back to back, you understand
this 2 wank night last night.
Some tossing a turning
and s-o-m-e 2 wank night yearning.

Couldn't sleep, mind past tired,
this wank in hand last night.
And I know what to do alright
on this 2 wank night last night.

A second dream, not a second episode
fulfilling my 2 wank dream night.
A new chapter, new players to excite
oh gosh, 2 hands needed for this second wank last night.

but I have to be up soon
will anyone know of my 2 wank night last night ?
Well if anyone guesses, I'll be bold, yet polite
YES YES I HAD 2 WANKS LAST NIGHT OL RIGHT !

My arms a bit tired.
Hummmm a 2 wank night tonight ?
Could be like my Kryptonight
fuck it yeah, its a 2 wank night tonight !

She is dead, long live She

Our relationship
just spent words
brushed into a corner
a carpenters wood chips and shavings

my counsel is dead
long live my counsel

once filled with vigour meaning and importance
now lie flat, deflated
awaiting the slow passing of time

my guardian spirit is dead
long live my guardian spirit

all those words,
unfathomable and eternal
nourished the world deprived of love

my pedestal is dead
long live my pedestal

all those emotions
bold enough to take on any army
now surrendered and lie face down

my shining light is dead
long live my shining light

the words will return to the earth
the meanings will degrade
and no one will remember

for my best friend is dead
long live my best friend

Pause Page

New towns edgy wash

Newtown's not so new town
built in obsolescence
awkward adolescence

quirky slipped to the beige
trademarks and copyright
it doesn't feel quite right

maybe it's me
I don't see edgy
no punks with eight inch Mohawks
no mad crazied junkies
no leather strapped gang-bang gay-boys

Newtown's not old town
but it's moved
yet small pockets of the great unwashed
still live, still alive and now own

the artist run galleries built on love and hope
replaced with art gallery like shops
Its safer, I don't get break ins
but there's no break-outs either

have I changed or
or did I change Newtown
its still left, still no right
but its less,
no marching in the street
no voting with you lungs and placards
placid edgy-less-ness for the masses

nightly smells wafts
imported for the bright light nights
scantily clad perfume and crisp buff aftershave
motto'd here for a good time, not a long time
cover themselves in Newtown's edgy wash
all the while destination Newtown shouts NSW tourism

disposable testosterone
mixed with
giggle packs of notice wanting girls
very after Insta gossip content

and where's the pot smoking hippy gone
with his cosmic kaftan
the skinny slightly smelly thing
with Jesus boots
no money
sucking you into some para-dime

rare are striking punk bleach hairs
more teal and green stop by
and let the corporate hairs down
and check out this latest bar-dish-venue

there's no dreads
no studded leather jackets
but there's a lot of tattoos
sleeves of them.
Tribal, single colour, pictures of mum or the phrase
or is this just the picture I see

30 years ago
McDonald was booted from here
only place in the world sent packing
now its franchised gelato

multi national sunglasses
fast fashion t shirts preaching green credentials
ha, green wash meets edgy wash

its not Newtown
its lost its punk
its lost its spunk
its ubertown
get it delivered in 20 minutes or its free
by a low paid non native speaking bike riding student
risking life with no lights or self care
edging toward a hint of back door migration

the smells have changed
its not fear or pot or doggy Chinese restaurant rubbish bins
its affluence
sometimes confused effluence
edgy has moved to passive
cutting edge has been replaced with the Ikea knife sharpener
bold has been replaced with a dinner meal deal
unconventional has been replaced with latte.

Is this Newtown
Is this my town
Or just me

not bad

not too bad
for a white fella
in a black country

www.ingramcontent.com/pod-product-compliance
Lightning Source LLC
Chambersburg PA
CBHW020451220526
45464CB00002B/949